21 GIRLS WHO MADE THE WORLD a Better Place

OLIVIA OMOTOSHO

21 GIRLS WHO MADE THE WORLD A BETTER PLACE

Olivia Omotosho

DOWNLOAD THE

'21 GIRLS WHO MADE THE WORLD A BETTER PLACE WORKBOOK' FREE

Yay... You have a GIFT!

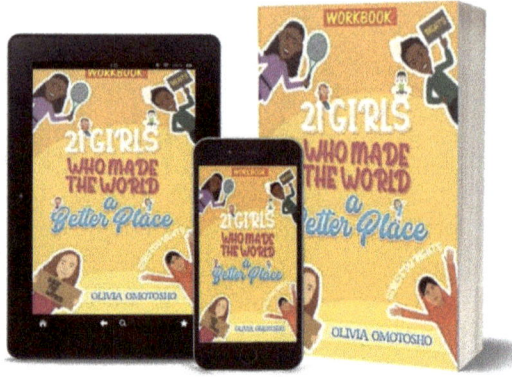

To specially thank you for purchasing this book, go to the link below to claim your FREE workbook!

http://eepurl.com/hmmKCv

OR

scan the QR code below

I would like to hear from all the amazing girls and boys who read the book and work through the workbook. If you have any questions, feedback or review, please feel free to reach out to me at **oliviaomotosho@gmail.com.**

Be great,

Olivia Omotosho.

21 GIRLS WHO MADE THE WORLD A BETTER PLACE

Copyright © 2020 by Olivia Omotosho

All rights reserved.

Requests for information should be addressed to:

oliviaomotosho@gmail.com

This book, or parts thereof, may not be reproduced, stored in a retrieval system, or transmitted in any form or by any means, electronic, mechanical, photocopying, recording or otherwise, without the written permission of the author.

The author would like to acknowledge the people illustrated in this book for becoming legends who made the world a better place and for inspiring girls all over the world. Although the author has made every effort to ensure that the information in this book was correct at press time, some events have been compressed and some dialogues have been recreated.

The author and the publisher do not assume and hereby disclaim any liability to any party for any loss, damage, or disruption caused by errors or omissions, whether such errors or omissions result from negligence, accident, or any other cause.

Published By: Achievers World Publishing, Australia.

ISBN: 978-0-6489792-0-3

Preface

I am Doyinsola Omotosho, and my preferred name is Olivia. I was born in Nigeria, then I moved to Australia when I was 4 and I have been here ever since. I have moved from state to state and Melbourne, in the state of Victoria is the third.

My dad always told me that I would change the world. My parents always encouraged me by saying, "You are going to be a superstar" or "You are amazing, and I love you." My dad has lots of books in his library and has read almost every single one of them - he is always encouraging me to read some of them as well. In 2018, my dad bought me a book called R for Rich life by Julie Davey. I read the whole book in just one day and I had never done that before. It was so good that I asked my dad if I could contact the author and of course, he happily said a great big YES! I wrote the letter after finding the address in a book. After the letter had been sent, I waited. Then one day, at the front door, I saw a gift and it was from Julie Davey! Inside of it was a letter and a book. My dad, my mum and I read the letter together. Julie's email address was on the letter, so we could contact her easily. We started talking to Julie Davey and even invited her over to my house. When the day for Julie Davey's visit arrived, I could barely concentrate on my schoolwork! When I got home from school,

Julie and her husband came almost instantly. We all had a nice talk before Julie left.

Julie also came to my school and had a talk with us all. She called out my name, and then I went to the stage to tell the story of how I got Julie to come to the school. I also talked about some of the books I had read. Among the books were two of Julie's works, titled:

1. R for Rich life

2. Attitude in Action

Another book that I read was 'Hannah's Christmas gift' by Bruce Sullivan, which was illustrated by Julie Davey. It was actually a business book and I was seven at the time. I told Julie that I wanted to write a book and here I am!

It's a wonder what books and hard work can do for you.

DEDICATION

I dedicate this book to my dad, my mum,

my little brother – Ifedayo.

And to Julie Davey and

All the amazing girls out there.

Contents

Ruby bridges 14
Malala Yousafzai 18
Alexandra Scott 22
Claudette Colvin 26
Bana Alabed 28
Capri Everitt 32
Yusra Mardini 36
Margaret E. Knight 40
Yuan Yuan Tan 44
Sylvia Mendez 48
Yara Shahidi 50
Sophie Cruz 54
Marley Dias 56
Barbara Johns 58
Thandiwe Chama 60
Samantha Smith 62
Mikaila Ulmer 68
Ann Makosinski 72
Elif Bilgin 74
Serena Williams 76
Coco Gauff 80
Olivia Omotosho 84

What People Are Saying About The Book

I give this book a 10/10 because it talks about strong girls who made a difference in society. My favourite would be Malala Yousafzai because she wanted every girl to talk when something is wrong. She survived bullets from the Taliban because she wanted every girl to go to have an education. But the Taliban only wanted boys to have an education. Now she lives as a happy Muslim lady all because of a book, a pen and a teacher. Thank you so much for this book. Best regards,
— *Felicia Iguodala*

Like the saying goes, "you are the company you keep". For a girl Olivia's age to have started keeping company with such great people as the 21 she mentioned in her book shows great potential which I'm sure will see her achieving great feats just like them. This is a book that a lot of young children can read to know what the great ladies have done and be inspired to set out and achieve something great also, because IT IS POSSIBLE.   — *Israel Orenuga*

21 girls who made the world a better place is such an inspiring book put together by the lovely Olivia. I'm privileged to know her, and I must say that this is an amazing read. I'd encourage parents to get this book for their teenagers as a go-to book to remind them that "Impossible is truly nothing".

— *Love Alabi*

It is organic and fresh and for all ages.   — *Ashlyn Paul*

"NO MATTER HOW YOUNG YOU ARE, YOU CAN ACHIEVE ANYTHING"

— OLIVIA OMOTOSHO

Ruby Bridges

Her name is Ruby Bridges. Let's have a little look into who Ruby is, when she was born and where she was born. Ruby is an American civil rights activist and was the very first African American to enter the all-white William Frantz Elementary school in 1960.

Ruby was born on the 8th of September in Tylertown Mississippi, United States. Ruby grew up on a farm with her mum, dad, grandma and grandpa. When Ruby was 6 years old, she took a big step and entered an all-white elementary school. Ruby grew up in the time when rights were not equal. Once Ruby was enrolled in the school, some white parents removed their children from the school and all of the teachers refused to teach Ruby, except for one - her name was Mrs. Barbara Henry. For over a year, only Mrs. Barbara taught Ruby. On the first day, Ruby and her mother had to stay in the principal's

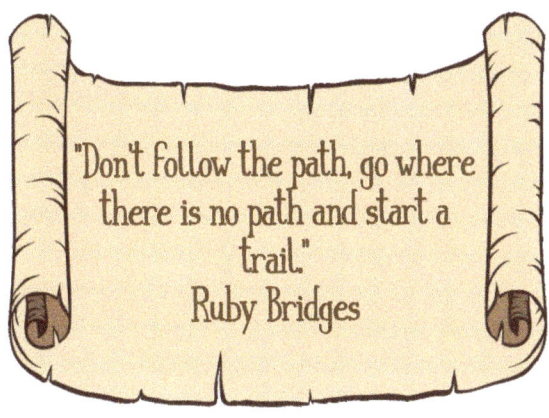
"Don't follow the path, go where there is no path and start a trail."
Ruby Bridges

office for the whole day because the chaos in the school stopped them from going to the classroom. As soon as Ruby entered, most of the others took their children out of the classroom but one white person broke the boycott and entered the school, saying, "I just want the privilege of taking my child to school." A few days after, other people started bringing their children to the school. Still, Ruby remained the only one in her class and this continued until the next year. Every morning when Ruby was walking to school, a woman would threaten to poison her while another held up a black baby doll in a coffin. Due to safety concerns, she was not allowed to eat the food from school - only the food that she got from her home. A child physicist called Robert Coles volunteered to give Ruby counselling and every week he would go to Ruby's home to check on her. Later on, he wrote a book — 'The Story of Ruby Bridges' to make everyone aware of her. The Bridges family really suffered as a result of the decision of taking Ruby to that school. Ruby's father lost his job as a gas station attendant and the store that the family always bought their groceries from would not allow them to shop there anymore. Ruby's grandparents who were sharecroppers, were also taken off their land. The family faced a whole lot more. A kind neighbour of theirs provided another job for Ruby's father.

Ruby stayed strong and worked hard on her education. Ruby became an education activist and a travel agent. She is an extraordinary girl who still lives today. She is about 65 years old and lives in New Orleans.

Malala Yousafzai

Malala Yousafzai is a very wonderful girl, so let's learn more about who she is. Malala is a Pakistani education advocate born on July 12, 1997. Malala is from Swat, Pakistan and her hometown is Mingora. This was during a time when girls were not allowed to go to school and get fully educated. However, Malala did not listen to those rules and went to school anyway. Instead, she fought for girls' education rights in Swat.

In the late 2008, Aamer Ahmed Khan, founder of the BBC Urdu website and his colleagues got the idea of asking a schoolgirl to blog anonymously about her life in Swat. Their correspondent from Peshawar, Abdul Hai Kakar, had been in touch with a local

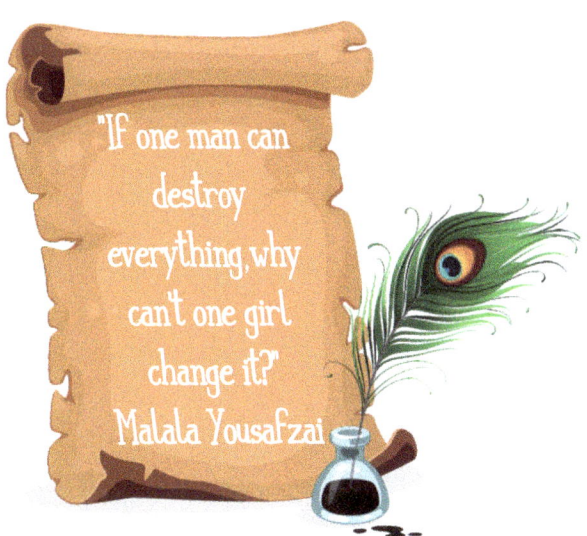

"If one man can destroy everything, why can't one girl change it?"
Malala Yousafzai

schoolteacher, Mr. Ziaudin Yousafzai (Malala's father). Mr. Ziaudin searched for a girl, but all was in vain as their parents thought of this plan as being extremely dangerous. Finally, Mr. Ziaudin mentioned 11-year-old Malala. At that time, Taliban militants were led by Maulana Fazlullah. They were taking over the Swat Valley, banning television, music, girls' education and women from going shopping. Bodies of beheaded policemen were being shown on the town square. Once, there was a girl from Mr. Ziaudin's school named Aisha who agreed to write a diary, but her parents soon stopped her because of the risks associated with it. The only alternative was Malala, who was 4 years younger than the original volunteer. Malala was in 7th grade at the time, so the editors at the BBC unanimously agreed. In Mingora, the Taliban had set an official ban that girls were not allowed to go to school, starting from 15 January 2009; they had already blown up more than 100 girls schools. The night before the ban took place, the air was filled with the noise of artillery gunfire and it woke Malala up several times. The Taliban destroyed several more schools and on January 24, 2009, Malala wrote this: 'Our annual exams are coming up. The exams are after the vacation but doing it will only be possible if the Taliban allows us girls to go to school. The teachers have told us to prepare for certain parts of the exam but I do not feel like studying.'

In February 2009, girls' schools were still closed. People had agreed that the private boys' schools would not open until 9th February and there were notices saying so. After the boys' schools reopened, the Taliban lifted the restrictions of girls' education. There was co-education and only 70 out of 700 girls were chosen to attend.

One day on her way home from school, after an exam, Malala was talking to her two friends about schoolwork when a Taliban shot three bullets at Malala. It was because she started school and that was against tradition. Many doctors in the town tried to help Malala but none of them could help, so she got transported to England and got treated at the Queen Elizabeth Hospital.

The doctors helped Malala, and she woke up from unconsciousness after a while. Later on, Malala went to school in England where the kids were extremely nice. That's how Malala became an education advocate. Malala stood by her word and continued her education.

Alexandra Scott

Alexandra Scott's story was emotional. We will call her Alex for short. Alex's story is very extraordinary because she made heaps of money from a small business and that probably saved hundreds of people's lives! Alex was born on 18th January 1996 in Manchester, Connecticut, United States.

A bit before her first birthday, Alex was diagnosed with Neuroblastoma. Everything was going smoothly until the next year when the heartbreaking finding reveals that Alex was growing tumours again! A day after her birthday, in 2000, Alex got a stem cell transplant. She told her mother, "When I get out of the hospital, I want to have a lemonade stand so that the doctors can help other kids just

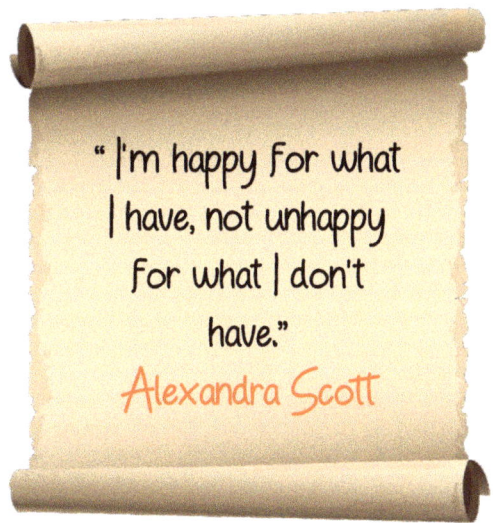

like they helped me." Later on that year, Alex had her first lemonade stand and further into the year with the help of her brother, Alex, made a whopping $2,000! The money was donated to charity to help cancer patients. In August 2004, Alex passed away at the age of eight. Alex did not make the money to enrich herself, but to help other kids with cancer to live a full and happy life.

Claudette Colvin

Claudette was born on September 5, 1939 in Montgomery, Alabama and lived in the poorer parts where there was a lot of segregation. Claudette stood up for herself even though she knew that there would be a huge consequence. She studied really hard and she even wanted to become president!

It all started when she was fifteen. On March 2, 1955, Claudette was riding home on a city bus when the bus driver told her to stand up for a white person. However, she did not listen and said, *"It's my right to sit here. I paid my fare, so I get to sit wherever I want to and there is no need for me to stand up for anyone whatsoever."*

They took her to prison because of this and she stayed there for several hours. After all those hours, she was finally free to go back to her family, who were so scared that they did not even sleep the night before! She is a truly wonderful person and is still alive.

> "I knew then and I know now, when it comes to justice, there is no easy way to get it."
>
> Claudette Colvin

Bana Alabed

Bana became an advocate for peace at a very young age. Bana was born on June 7, 2009 to a learned family; Bana's mum is a teacher and her dad is a lawyer. She is from Aleppo, Syria. When Bana was 7, a war began. Glass shattered, buildings were crushed, and before long, her SCHOOL WAS BOMBED!! Oh, what a horrible sight it was! Afterwards, Bana joined Twitter and on that app, she pleaded that the war should stop!

Her mom still wanted her to have an education, so they fled from Aleppo to Turkey, after their home was bombed. Not long after, she started

"The world can do better and be kinder to refugees. We are innocent. Refugees need homes, jobs and education. Especially the children because education is our right. Without education, our future is lost and we can't grow up to make the world better from what we've learned and take care of other people and our families."

Bana Alabed

school again and her dreams to be a teacher lit up again, and now, she is having a very good education. Bana is still very active on Twitter, where she tweets about things happening in Syria and how people can be of help. All Bana wants is peace; peace in Syria and peace all around the world. Bana did her best in trying to stop the war; she played an extremely big role in it.

Capri Everitt

Capri was born on August 30, 2004 in Canada. She did an amazing job by achieving a really big goal that took a lot of practise and hard work. She has a Guinness world record for singing 80 different national anthems, from different countries and in 41 languages - all within 1 year! Capri had one goal on her mind during the 1 year: to raise money to help orphaned and abandoned children.

Capri was inspired by the book, 'The world needs your kid', by Craig Keilbuger. She asked herself, "What is a song everyone in the country would know? Ah ha! - The national anthem!" And so, her family started preparing for trips to 80 countries around the globe because Capri wanted to sing the anthems in the language! During this time, Capri and her brother, Bowen, had to keep up with schoolwork, so they planned out everything before they started their

journey. They also brought along textbooks. After the long trip, Capri got a world record for the most national anthems sung in one year! Capri was very grateful to her parents who raised money for her trips by selling their cars and renting out their house. Capri had a big idea and a wonderful family to support it.

Yusra Mardini

Yusra was born on March 5, 1998 and she is from Darayya, Syria. Yusra will be remembered for using her talent to help people in need. There was a Syrian civil war and this led to Yusra's house getting destroyed! Yusra, her sister and a few other people fled Syria, and she saved a bunch of people after the engine of the boat they were travelling on stopped working. Because she could swim,

Yusra joined some other people to push the boat for about three hours! After that, they found a small piece of land. However, she did not always love swimming! When she was 3, her dad wanted her to swim but she refused. Her dad had pushed her in the water several times and she eventually learned despite her gasping for air each time.

> "The most important thing in my life is swimming, and then speaking and doing things to help refugees."
>
> Yusra Mardini

When they arrived in Germany, Yusra looked for the closest swimming pool around and after a lot of focused, hard work, Yusra became an Olympic swimmer. Yusra is indeed an amazing girl.

Margaret E. Knight

Margaret was born on February 14, 1838 in York, Maine. Her father died when she was young, so Margaret's family went to Manchester, New Hampshire. She received a good education but had to leave to work in a cotton mill. So many times, Margaret used her understanding of machines to help people when required.

At age 12, while she was observing her brothers doing work in a cloth factory, she saw a metal tipped shuttle shot out of the loom, exposing a worker to severe danger. This incident influenced Margaret to construct a stop motion device to forestall loom accidents. It was later also adopted by other Manchester mills. In her teens and early 20's,

> "I was always making things for my brothers; did they want anything in the line of play, they always said, "Mattie will make them for us". I was famous for my kites; my sleds were the envy and admiration of all boys in town."
>
> Margaret E. Knight

she took several other jobs such as home repair, photography and engraving. As an adult, Margaret moved to Springfield, Massachusetts to work for a manufacturer of paper bags. After studying this work, she made a machine that produced square based paper bags, so that it would make it possible for people to burden the bag without holding it upright. Two years after that, Margaret started to add the finishing touches to the paper bag machine so that it could be patented.

Margaret died on October 12, 1914 at the age of 76. She was an amazing girl.

Yuan Yuan Tan

Yuan was born on the 14th of February 1977; she is from Shanghai, China. When Yuan was 5, she became interested in ballet when she watched a broadcast of Galina Ulanova performing Swan Lake. She kept an interest in ballet throughout her primary years and at the age of 10, she was chosen by the Shanghai ballet school!

However, Yuan's father did not want her to have ballet as a career. Thankfully, what her mother wanted was the exact opposite. So, to choose whom Yuan was going to listen to, they flipped a 5-fen coin - her mother won. Yuan won many international awards at a young age: including a gold medal and the Nijinsky award. At 18 years old, she became a soloist at the San Francisco ballet company. Two years

"Perfect one thing at a time."
Yuan Yuan Tan

later, in 1997, Yuan was promoted to principal ballet dancer! This was the highest position a dancer could get and it was very rapid growth for Yuan as she was very young. She was the youngest principal dancer ever recorded in the history of the San Francisco ballet company! And so, Yuan Yuan Tan became a famous ballet dancer. Yuan tried out something new and worked on it with a lot of commitment.

Sylvia Mendez

Sylvia was born on June 7th, 1936 in Santa Ana, California. Sylvia's family had just moved to Westminster. In the 1940s, there were some troubles as there were only two schools around: Hoover elementary school and 17th street elementary school. Sylvia's parents wanted to get Sylvia, her two brothers and their cousins into the 17th street elementary but they were rejected. It was an all white school and also did not allow people that were Hispanic. Her cousins who were light-skinned were accepted, but not Sylvia and her brothers as they were dark-skinned and had a Hispanic surname. This made Sylvia's aunt very angry and she stormed out of the school in a rage.

On January 19, 1948 they were finally allowed to attend the 17th street elementary, hence becoming the first Hispanic in an all-white school in California. It was hard for Sylvia and her siblings as her peers called her names and treated her badly. But she got through it and became a successful nurse. Sylvia fought for her right to be enrolled in a school of her choice and she had an amazing family to support her along the way.

That was the story of Sylvia Mendez.

"My parents just wanted what was best for their children."
Sylvia Mendez

Yara Shahidi

Yara was born on February 10, 2000, in Minneapolis, Minnesota, U.S. Yara has a brother and a sister. Yara found her talent and built it up, starting from featuring in magazines to movies!

When she was 4, her family moved to California and when she was 6, she started appearing on advertisements and posters for places like McDonald's. Yara made her cinematic debut in 2009, where she played Olivia Danielson, in the movie *Imagine That* and she won The Young Artist Award! She also appeared in the action movie *Salt* alongside Angelina Jolie, in 2010. Yara acted as Chloe Johnson, daughter of President William Johnson in 2012 then in the movie *Black-ish* in 2014, *Grown-ish* in 2018 and *'the sun is also a star'* in

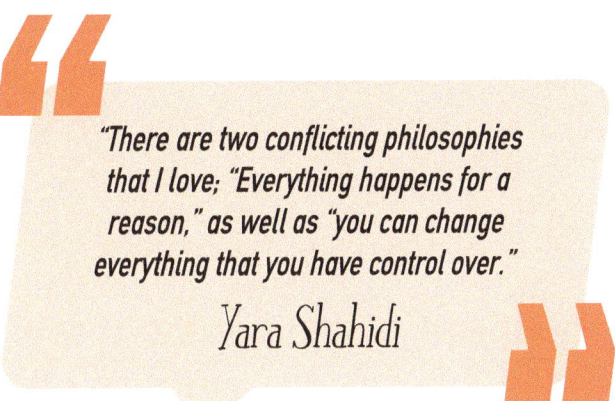

"There are two conflicting philosophies that I love; "Everything happens for a reason," as well as "you can change everything that you have control over."

Yara Shahidi

2019. She was also one of the 15 women who were chosen to appear on the 2019 magazine issue of British Vogue.

Yara also founded *'eighteen X 18'*, hoping to end poverty.

Yara is now 20 years old. She is a very good actress and I hope to meet her one day!

Sophie Cruz

Sophie fought for what is right. In 2015, Sophie was 5. She went to see Pope Francis when he was visiting Washington to attend to the immigrants. Sophie is an immigrant from Mexico. That same day, she wore a shirt that said, "PAPA Rescate DAPA," thus pushing the Pope to support the deferred action for parents of Americans.

When the Pope's car passed by the street, Sophie ran down the road to see him but was turned away by security. But the Pope had seen her run out of the crowd and requested to meet Sophie. He hugged her and when she told him everything, the Pope declared a meeting, encouraging greater openness for immigrants and refugees. In 2016, Sophie was invited by President Barrack Obama at the White House for a Cinco de Mayo celebration. Sophie always fought for the people who were living in poverty and if she saw someone, she would always try to find a way to help them. That was how she became an American activist.

"Let us fight with love, faith and courage so that our families will not be destroyed."

Sophie Cruz

Marley Dias

Marley is an American activist and feminist, born January 3, 2005, in Philadelphia but grew up in New Jersey. She was also named after a reggae singer, Bob Marley! When Marley was 11, she complained to her mother that all of her mandatory books were all about white boys and dogs, so there wasn't any freedom for her to read what she wanted. After talking to her mother, she decided to make a book drive '#1000BlackGirlBooks'. Marley observed what was wrong and saw what she could change and changed it.

In 2017, Marley won the Smithsonian Magazine's American Ingenuity Award in the Youth category. Her book drive is based on books in which the main character is a black girl. Marley's goal was to collect and donate 1000 books to black girls. Many of the books were sent to a children's book drive in Jamaica. The campaign also called for public concentration on the absence of diversity in children literature. Marley has her own book now, too!

Marley Dias is an amazing girl indeed!

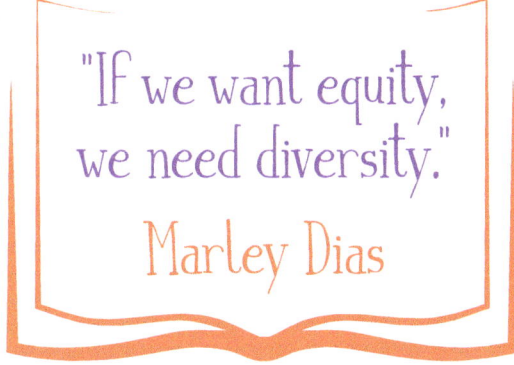

"If we want equity, we need diversity."
Marley Dias

Barbara Johns

Barbara was born on March 6, 1935, in New York City, but grew up in Prince Edward County, Virginia.

Barbara's mother worked in Washington D.C for the U.S Navy, and her father worked on a farm. She was educated in segregated public schools. Across town, there was another school but it was only for white people. In winter, the school was very cold, so they had to wear their jackets every day! The pupils that sat closest to the wooden stove were cosy and warm while the students who sat farthest from the stove were freezing! When it rained, they would get water in the classroom, and there were buckets everywhere! Barbara was tired of missing the school bus and watching all the white people getting on theirs and leaving her alone to wait, and decided she had to put a stop to it!

Barbara went to a trusted teacher to discuss her plan. She also met with a few of her friends and they agreed to help her organize a students' strike! They persuaded the principal into going for an event to address some of his students were causing trouble. After the principal left, Barbara and her friends actioned their strike plans. After the strike, Barbara went to live with her uncle. Barbara made sure that she got a good school with very good conditions.

"We had talents and abilities...that weren't really being realised."
— Barbara Johns

Thandiwe Chama

Thandiwe is a Zambian girl. When she was 8, her school had to close because there were no teachers. But she could not take it; she needed to do something!

So, she led 60 other children to find another school. Not long after, the children were taken to the Jack Cecup School. All the children supported her along the way. She was strengthened by her achievement and therefore, she continues to fight for the right of children education. Thandiwe will always be remembered for leading a lot of people in search for another school at a very young age.

"Every child has the right to live and that is the right for life."

Thandiwe Chama

Samantha Smith

Samantha was born in Houlton Maine, the U.S. on June 29, 1972. Samantha's goal was to stop world wars and to make peace with everyone.

Her family settled in Manchester, Maine, when Samantha finished second grade and there, she went to Manchester Elementary School. In November 1982, Samantha wrote a letter to Soviet leader, Yuri Andropov, saying:

Dear Mr. Andropov,

My name is Samantha Smith. I am ten years old. Congratulations on your new job. I have been worrying about Russia and the United States getting into a nuclear war. Are you going to vote to have a war or not? If you aren't, please tell me how you are going to help to not have a war. This question you do not have to answer, but I would like to know why you want to conquer the world or at least our country. God made the world for us to live together in peace and not to fight.

Sincerely,

Samantha Smith

Samantha was happy to know that her letter was published in the newspaper! But wasn't so happy when he didn't reply. So, she sent a letter to the Soviet Union's ambassador to the United States asking if Andropov had responded.

The next year, Samantha received a response:

Dear Samantha,

I received your letter, which is like many others that have reached me recently from your country and from other countries around the world.

It seems to me — I can tell by your letter — that you are a courageous and honest girl, resembling Becky, the friend of Tom Sawyer in the famous book of your compatriot, Mark Twain. This book is well-known and loved in our country by all boys and girls.

You write that you are anxious about whether there will be a nuclear war between our two countries. And you ask if we are doing anything so that war will not break out.

Your question is the most important of those that every thinking man can pose. I will reply to you seriously and honestly.

Yes, Samantha, we in the Soviet Union are trying to do everything so that there will not be war on Earth. This is what every Soviet man wants. This is what the great founder of our state, Vladimir Lenin, taught us.

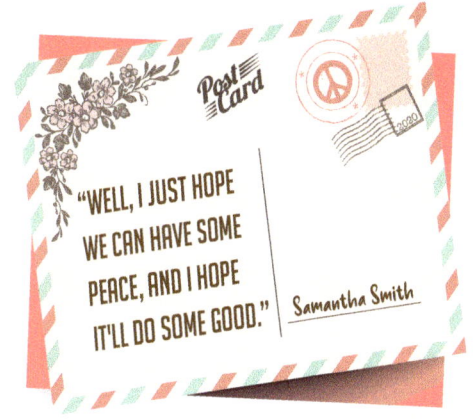

Soviet people well know what a terrible thing war is. Forty-two years ago, Nazi Germany, which strove for supremacy over the whole world, attacked our country, burned and destroyed many thousands of our towns and villages, killed millions of Soviet men, women and children.

In that war, which ended with our victory, we were in alliance with the United States: together we fought for the liberation of many people from the Nazi invaders. I hope that you know about this from your history lessons in school. And today, we want very much to live in peace, to trade and cooperate with all our neighbours on this earth — with those far away and those nearby. And certainly, with such a great country as the United States of America.

In America and in our country, there are nuclear weapons — terrible weapons that can kill millions of people in an instant. But we do not want them to be ever used. That's precisely why the Soviet Union solemnly declared throughout the entire world that never — never — will it use nuclear weapons first against any country. In general, we propose to discontinue further production of them and to proceed to the abolition of all the stockpiles on Earth.

It seems to me that this is a sufficient answer to your second question: 'Why do you want to wage war against the whole world or at least the United States?' We want nothing of the kind. No one in our country — workers, peasants, writers nor doctors, neither grown-ups nor children, nor members of the government — want either a big or 'little' war.

We want peace — there is something that we are occupied with: growing wheat, building and inventing, writing books and flying into space. We want peace for ourselves and for all peoples of the planet. For our children and for you, Samantha.

I invite you, if your parents will let you, to come to our country, the best time being this summer. You will find out about our country, meet with your contemporaries, visit an international children's camp — Artek — on the sea. And see for yourself: in the Soviet Union, everyone is for peace and friendship among peoples.

Thank you for your letter. I wish you all the best in your young life.

Y. Andropov

Samantha went to Moscow with her parents on July 7, 1983 and spent two weeks there. She went to Artek, but she did not meet Yuri Andropov himself because he had fallen very ill but they spoke on the telephone. Samantha also spoke with the first woman to orbit the earth, Valentina Tereshkova. Unfortunately, not knowing who she was talking to, Samantha mistakenly hung up after only a small conversation. Samantha died on August 25, 1985, because of a plane crash.

Samantha was truly an incredible girl.

Mikaila Ulmer

Mikaila is a 13-year-old-girl who has her own business! Makaila used something as small as a bee, turned it into an experiment, and made a career out of it! It all started when Mikaila was 4. In one week, she got stung by two bees and it was really painful. She was terrified of bees but her mother turned this into a learning opportunity about insects. Mikaila learnt that bees could possibly become extinct, and humans would only live for 4 more years. So, later on, she started a lemonade stand, but instead of using sugar, she used organic honey.

Mikaila's company is growing and she has even created new flavours! She is also sending most of the money to organizations to save the honeybees. Mikaila went from being scared of bees to giving space to keep them. Her lemonade has been stocked in 500 stores!

"You can't expect great things to happen if you don't work for them."
— Mikaila Ulmer

She has to balance her school life and work life, so if there is a big test at school, she will have to skip a big interview. Or if there is a big interview, she will have to miss school! She said, 'It's not the easiest for sure.'

Mikaila is an amazing girl.

Ann Makosinski

Ann was born on October 3, 1997. Ann is of Filipino, Polish, and Canadian descent. She studied at St. Michaels University School. For her 7th grade project, Ann invented a radio that can be powered by a candle; she also made a piezoelectric flashlight when she was in 9th grade.

In 2013, when Ann was 16, she won the Google science fair. She invented the hollow flashlight. It is a flashlight that is powered by body heat, getting the inspiration from when she visited the Philippines where her friend failed high school because of a lack of electricity; they couldn't study at night.

Ann is still alive today, probably creating new things.

"I think everything starts with an Idea. No matter how crazy it is, you should always try to bring it to life."

Ann Makosinski

Elif Bilgin

Elif is a young genius. Elif was born in 1997 in Istanbul, Turkey. At the age of 4, Elif taught herself how to read and write, so that way she could also read science books. As you can see, Elif is always very eager to learn. Elif used something that we throw away in our everyday life, and turned it into something extraordinary! Her very first invention was making window wipers for her glasses.

When Elif was 14, there was a lot of pollution going on in Turkey, and she really wanted to help reduce it. So, she began her new invention to make bioplastic out of banana peels. Elif worked on this project for 2 years and did 12 experiments: in which 10 failed. But after finally being successful with 2 experiments, she entered it into the 2013 Google science fair competition. In September of 2013, Elif was declared the winner. She was a guest speaker at many different conferences.

Elif Bilgin truly is a gifted girl.

"The first step to getting what you want is having courage to get rid of what you don't."

Elif Bilgin

Serena Williams

Serena Williams is a famous tennis player who has won a lot of tennis matches. Let's learn more about her.

Serena was born on September 26, 1981 in Michigan, United States. Serena is the youngest of her 5 siblings. When the children were young, they moved to Compton, California and that was where Serena started playing tennis at 4 years old. Her father homeschooled Serena and Venus, her older sister. When Serena was 9, she moved with her family to West Palm beach, Florida, so that Serena could attend the tennis academy of Rick Macci. Serena's father stopped sending her and her sister to the tennis tournaments when Serena was 10 so that they could focus on their schoolwork.

"When you lose you get up, you make it better, and you try again."
Serena Williams

Racism also influenced this experience because Serena's dad heard some other people talking about Serena and Venus disrespectfully while playing tennis. They went to school and Serena continued playing tennis and became the star we know today.

Serena Williams is an amazing person and has experienced a lot of wins.

Coco Gauff

Coco was born on March 13, 2004, in Delray Beach, Florida.

She has two younger brothers, Cody and Cameron. Coco first developed an interest in tennis at age 4 while watching Serena Williams win at the 2009 Australian open but her parents always told her to try a wide range of sports. She started tennis at 6 years old and decided to become a famous tennis star. She loved tennis because it was an individual sport and she did very well at it. At 10 years old, Coco started to train at the Mouratoglou academy, where Serena Williams trained. Her coach was extremely impressed by her and she continued to have success! She won the USTA Clay Court National for age 12 and under. At that time, Coco was 10 years and 3

"Obviously, there's always room for improvement."

Coco Guaff

months old when she won! She became the youngest champion in the tournament's history! Coco is a former world number 1 junior player and is the youngest player to make it to the top 100 in the Women's Tennis Association (WTA).

Coco Gauf is an extremely extraordinary girl!

Olivia Omotosho

Girls

Roses are red,
Girls are cool
Just like blue violets,
And you know that too

Sun flowers are yellow,
Girls are nice
Just like regal white lilies,
And you know that's right

Roses are red,
Girls are awesome
Just like bouquets of daisies,
And you know that's true

Tulips are colorful,
Girls are beautiful
Just like green palm leaves
And that's how we roll.

Olivia Omotosho - Poem, 2020

OLIVIA OMOTOSHO

ISBN 9780648979203

www.ingramcontent.com/pod-product-compliance
Lightning Source LLC
Chambersburg PA
CBHW051540010526
44107CB00064B/2791